FERN-TEXTS

ALSO BY REGINALD GIBBONS

The Ruined Motel (poetry)
Saints (poetry)
Maybe It Was So (poetry)
Sparrow (poetry)
Homage to Longshot O'Leary (poetry)
It's Time (poetry)
In the Warhouse (poetry)
Sweetbitter (novel)
Five Pears or Peaches (stories)
Selected Poems of Luis Cernuda (translation)
Bakkhai (translation, with Charles Segal)
Antigone (translation, with Charles Segal)
The Poet's Work: 29 Poets on the Origins and Practice of Their Art (editor)

FERN-TEXTS
Autobiographical Essay on the Notebooks of Young S. T. Coleridge (b. 1772)

A Chapbook

Reginald Gibbons

Hollyridge Press
Venice, California

© 2005 REGINALD GIBBONS

All rights reserved under International and Pan-American Copyright Conventions. Published in the United States by Hollyridge Press.

Hollyridge Press
P.O. Box 2872
Venice, California 90294
www.hollyridgepress.com

Cover and Book Design by Rio Smyth
Author photo by Cornelia Maude Spelman
Cover photos:
Detail from "San Francisco from Headlands" by Don Mace (Dreamstime.com)
"Sunset Colors" by Radu Razvan (Dreamstime.com)
Manufactured in the United States of America by Lightning Source

ISBN-13: 978-0-9772298-3-3
ISBN-10: 0-9772298-3-1

12 11 10 09 08 07 06 05   10 9 8 7 6 5 4 3 2 1

FERN-TEXTS
Autobiographical Essay
on the Notebooks of
Young S. T. Coleridge
(b. 1772)

1.

Coleridge wrote of himself:

> There are two sorts of talkative fellows whom it would be injurious to confound
>
> & I, S. T. Coleridge, am the latter. The first sort is of those who use five hundred words more [than] there needs to express an idea—that is not my case—few men, I will be bold to say, put more meaning into their words than I or choose them more deliberately & discriminatingly. The second sort is of those who use five hundred more ideas, images, reasons &c than there is any need of to arrive at their object
>
> till the only object arrived at is that the mind's eye of the bye-stander is dazzled with colors succeeding so rapidly as to leave one vague impression that there has been a great Blaze of colours all about something. Now this is my case—& a grievous fault it is
>
> my illustrations swallow up my thesis
> [25 December 1804]

But begin with metaphor:

> Ginger to be sliced—Lemons to be peeled—The Sugar & Water to be boiled together, & the Scum—viz—the Monarchical part [—] must go to Pot—and out of the Pot—*Then* put in the Ginger with the Peels of the Lemons, and let the whole be boiled together gently for half an hour—When cold, put in the Lemon juice strained &c—then let the Sum total be

/ 3

put in the Barrel with three spoonfuls of Yeast—let it work three Days (Sundays Excepted—) and then put in a Gallon Barrel—Close up the Barrel—Nota bene—you may do it legally the habeas corpus act being suspended—let it remain a fortnight then bottle it.

[1795-6?]

(One could *tyrannically*
                        confine the fermenting stuff
because in '94 the
                        government had suspended
the right of persons not to
                        be jailed without being charged.)

2.

"Love transforms the souls into
             a conformity with the
object loved—" And when I too   [1796?]
             was twenty-four I had my   [1971]
own experience of such self-
             transformation that I could
not yet seize or recognize—
             experience of objects loved
but also feared, approving
             and disapproving: women,
men, cities, books, ideas,
             wearying labor, wild free-
dom in cars, America,
             how a people should govern
themselves, and war; and I tried
             to think every day about
what seemed unthinkable since
             it was so everyday: Dad,
for instance, working out of
             his car; Mother ordering
us all around and being
             ordered at her job; drinking
fountains and restrooms marked for
             race; barbed wire, tear gas, school, church,
a book shop, ditches, weeds, rain;
             often I had unconscious-
ly made myself adjust the
             goal in myself that I could
not myself perceive but which
             I longed to attain, reform-
ing it repeatedly in
             order to discover what
it might be or might become.

/ 5

                        He wrote: "An eminently
beautiful Object is Fern,
                on a hill side, scattered thick
but growing single—and all
                        shaking themselves in the wind." [August 1800]
"There have been times when looking
                up beneath the shelt[e]ring Tree,
I could Invest every leaf
                with Awe." From such words I make [September 1803]
the Samuel who will to
                me speak what I am able
to hear—a man excited
                to notice, describe, and love
no less than an explorer
                of America, the free
expanses that come into
                his view—in a landscape, in
an idea: they rise further
                into sight with each step up-
ward over a difficult
                pass, they rise with a kind of
magnificence we should not
                call "majestic" (remember
monarchical sugar): the
                view is of infinity,
as in the mere intricate
                veins of a leaf or one tree
of leaves or in the rushing
                stream of changeable feeling
at a farewell or a birth.
                I hold close in thought the work,
the writer, who will evoke
                in me what I want to be.

3.

Because of my own slow green
                passage toward freer thinking
I leave aside his hopes of
                Christianity (he'd be
horrified at this), and all
                the pretty rituals and
the austere, too, and willful
                ignorance and anger—yet
to say this in our culture
                is still to be subject to
denunciation by the
                theatrically faithful.
Yet how violently our own
                religions of conquest have
veered, how murderous and how
                self-acquitting they've been, how
agile and empty when they
                fix interpretation of
laws and signs they claim are theirs,
                in war and violation.
Young faithfulness evoked in
                me something good. Bad too, no
surprise, especially hot
                certainties I heard professed
by those around me. To be
                evoked as I wanted to
be—those values too, half learned
                from unhappy churchgoing—
I needed to choose other
                thinking, others. "My nature
requires another nature
                for its support"—not systems   [November 1803]
of thought or belief but re-

                    sponsive imagination
that becomes the very same
                    puzzling "*streamy* Nature of
Association" that Sam
                    believed "Thinking[, which] =
Reason[,] curbs & rudders." *Must*
                    curb, since Association,
to him, is "the Origin
                    of moral Evil." Like us   [December 1803]
he dreamed by day, following
                    the pleasure or the trouble
of leaping from thought to thought,
                    image to image. And he
himself knows that we grow up
                    "from Infancy to Manhood
under Parents, Schoolmasters,
                    Tutors, Inspectors," and more,
"having had our pleasures &
                    pleasant self-chosen Pursuits
interrupted, & we forced"
                    into what he says are "dull
unintelligible Rud-
                    iments or painful Labor."   [10 January 1804]
What teachers and masters in-
                    terrupted was his, our, soul-
making reverie, even
                    ethics of choice and being
chosen by what both frees and
                    affiliates us and gives
strength to leaping aid and calm
                    compassion. But Coleridge
locates moral lapsing in
                    the very reverie to
which he himself inclined, while
                    at the same time he grasps how
he needs such streamy thinking

                        to form himself as a man
with a conscience pained by his
                        own failings. He wonders "when
men shall be as proud within
                        themselves of having remained
an hour in a state of deep
                        tranquil Emotion, whether
in reading or in hearing
                        or in looking, as they now
are in having figured a-
                        way one hour." One supposes   [10-11 January 1804]
he is abominating
                        tallies of profit and loss,
those figures, yet one does hear
                        in his way of putting it
his saying what the poet
                        does: a figuring. His plan
of self-improvement followed:
                        "1 Up—wash—ginger Tea hot.
2 Italian till Breakfast
                        Time. 3 Breakfast 4 Write or
transcribe my Journal. 5th read
                        the Theodicee & take
notes for my Consolations.
                        6th Then write my letters on
literary Detraction
                        or a review of Wordsworth";

he added: "in short, something,
                        beginning with this. 7th
between dinner & tea what
                        I can. Read some Italian
if possible. after tea
                        till bed time try to compose."

/ 9

Final plea: "God grant me fort-
                titude & a perseuer-
ant Spirit of Industry!"—   [April 6, 1804]
                writing this while on a ship
bound for Malta and, he hoped,
                a position and an es-
cape from his misery at
                home: in love with a woman
not his wife and not in love
                with his wife, although yes dot-
ing on his small son and no
                not seeming to expect he'd
write more poems, and revising
                his own lived life history
as one who had acted a
                revolutionary (called
in England, "Jacobin") but
                now was deceiving others
and himself, defender of
                order and obedience,
God, sceptre, commentary.
                Increasingly an anti-
democratic man who'd come
                to hate those in whose name he'd
fought—yet he didn't have to
                like what common people did,
but only identify
                himself with their suffering,
no? He can't help but still *see*:

    Wednesday, April 11, 1804
    Sea & Sky, & an irregular circle of Ships of which we seem the Center. Saw a nice black faced bright black-eyed white toothed Boy running up to the Main Top with a large Leg of

Mutton swung, Albatross-fashion about his neck 'Rear'd' for a Ship lad, taught every thing by Curses—yet well-behav'd the while, & his Master shed a tear when he died—for the Boy would sing on the Top Mast, a Song neither of Love nor of Wine, & come down with Tears on his Cheeks

(Was the boy's racing up the
                        mast to the main top merely
high spirits? Or could he have
                        been escaping in order
to eat in freedom the meat
                        he had stolen, from hunger?
How did he happen to die?
                        For what reason did he die?)

The ethical—not only
                        to see but also to act.

4.

C. wrote down that Poetry
                    might be "a rationalized
Dream dealing [?out] to mani-
                        fold Forms our own Feelings, that
never perhaps were attached
                    by us consciously to our
own personal Selves." The wit
                    of poems, their arguments, all
that age-old manner of how
                    thought might move reasonably
in them, he saw was at heart
                    a dreaming, with states and shifts
of feeling and image and
                    narratives moving with that
peculiar syntax of con-
                    nections that lie beneath what
we think we think. Wasn't this   [11 May 1804]
                    his own discovery that
writing makes possible an
                    understanding of how we
should act, could claim our selves, must
                    redeem our selves from the acts
by which we have pawned ourselves,
                    from the formation that we
mistakenly accepted
                    or helplessly accepted
(formation, though, that we are
                    continuing to accept,
it is so hard to master)
                    as our servitude? Sailors
on several ships in his
                    convoy shot repeatedly
at an exhausted hawk that

                    tried to rest on the bowsprits,
that flew away each time but
                    had to return to rest on
one ship or another: "Poor
                    Hawk! O Strange Lust of Murder
in Man! It is not cruelty
                    it is mere non-feeling from
non-thinking." Pity for the
                    hawk, anguish; for the sailors
not distaste, hate, fear—in him
                    who had envisioned the shoot-
ing of the albatross!—but
                    fellow-feeling, forgiveness.

5.

Co-creating with other
             poets the new way in which
poetry in English would
             mostly work, he perceived the
linguistic spirit which (be-
             cause of the particular
history, customs, and thought
             of the English—and he would
have understood these in yet
             another way if his plans
of emigrating to this
             America had not failed)
had made possible in past
             poetry (and was feeding
the use by new poets of)
             "rapid associations
of sensuous images,"
             "rapid association
& combination both of
             images with images,
& of images, & com-
             binations of images[,]
with the moral and intel-
             lectual world, and vice ver-
sa[,] words of passion and thought
             with natural images."   [4-7 February 1805]

So that in him (and in Words-
             worth) we see those first moments
of a perceiving that's an

14 /

                        act sufficient to itself—
we read their early work in
                        the hope that this perceiving
won't become a *substitute*
                        for their democratic hopes
and a retreat from their friends
                        who are being chased through the
shires by zealous, triumphant
                        reactionaries into
persecuted hiding, jail...
                        But already we know the
story—Coleridge and Words-
                        worth will change. Yet they saw that
the poetic perceiving
                        is of some object—thing or
place, prospect or person—and
                        that the perceiving of a
person is an attending
                        to particular features,
qualities: ordinary,
                        concrete, specific, worn, real.
Then a poem needs no appeal
                        to divine sanction, nor to
an aristocratic nor
                        even a middle-class sense
of propriety, it needs
                        image and narration, it
needs the evocation of
                        another human being
in individuated
                        encounter, the poem needs a
conviction of uniqueness
                        and a tone of voice as if
whispering praise and sorrow,
                        language attuned to spicules,
sepals and scars, to surprise

                        that pleasingly confounds ex-
pectation, an attentive-
                        ness that at least sometimes thrills
to the strange, the sublimely
                        peculiar and to the im-
ponderable and the un-
                        conscious, what's this?? a grasping

(flawed by its wanting to know
                        everything and to possess)

graspable—and once I too   [1969-71]
                        went naming things, sensations,
and extending sentences
                        out to greater length as I
reached the wave-beaten New-World
                        west coast, where syntax too seemed
a wave to be caught, ridden,
                        "articulate energy,"
I started reading Duncan,
                        Rexroth, Levertov, Snyder,
in those days, Antoninus—
                        war, resistance, unarmed, armed,
talk-fights, hot hearts, chants, stands on
                        streets against cops and fragrant
stands of laurel on hillsides,
                        eucalyptus along roads,
sloping apricot orchards,
                        avocets on the wide beach
striding, beaking through each wave's
                        last thin rushing, and herons
in treetop nests, terns diving
                        with tucked wings and spearpoint plunge,
used books and records, good wine

                        sold cheap from stout oak barrels,
endless blossoming in yards,
                        woods, fields, gardens, bedrooms; and
incense burning in the streets—
                        but now my illustrations
will swallow up my thesis.
                        Which is: love capable of
affiliation and in-
                        dependence: love that could say
love, that could reform the mind
                        "into conformity with":
a Coast Range peak (that other,
                        western Black Mountain I hiked),
to seas chaotically
                        breaking against and into
rocks, caves, cliffs, thoughts—thoughts winging
                        fast as songbirds into mist
nets of larger thoughts that held
                        them only a moment, near
wet seaside fields of pumpkins
                        incandescent in fog-glow...

Music (not my own) in the   [1971-72]
                        family carried me out:
sped by just enough resolve
                        and by money from L.A.
where Uncle Dan with fiddle
                        had earned it in studios
and sent a check by airmail,
                        I lit out for the past, took
a long sea-journey: reading
                        Moby Dick in a sling chair
on the freight deck, playing chess
                        with two old spinster sisters

who both beat me happily,
               the course set not for Malta
but with cargo for Tangiers,
               then Civitavecchia; then
after disembarcation
               I crossed in a chugging mal-
functioning automobile
               overland through Italy
with V., in love with her, in
               love with the travel itself:
Croatia, Bosnia, coast lands,
               Kosovo, Montenegro,
then Greece and Turkey. Back west-
               ward again, to Venice, west
to Spain, and everywhere rich
               life and ruins, spies, soldiers, crushed
histories of uprisings,
               unrepaired bullet holes from
long ago in Madrid as
               in East Berlin, pocks of night
executions in stucco
               whitewashed village and roadside
walls of Andalucía,
               yet also, by grace, luck, strength,
and courage to resist, wine-
               celebrated survival;
Cernuda, Lorca, Hikmet,
               I read, I read Vallejo,
Neruda, Celan. A year
               later the return trip, by
ship again, through icebergs this
               time to thick disorderly
democratic spruce, maple,
               beech and birch forests of cold
northeastern America,
               colossus, then all the way

west overland in the same
                    stuttering car again to
the Pacific, but in my
                    case *not* having invented
a new way of writing, think-
                    ing or dreaming, in fact not
able to grasp, although I
                    could sense it just beyond reach,
a new understanding of
                    our time of beginnings, ends.

6.

[1972] In February in a small rented house standing alone amid grapefruit groves near the southeast coast of Spain, in the province of Murcia, V. and I had stayed with friends for a week, listening at night to mice overhead in the ceiling playing soccer with a kernel of corn; we were talking, eating and drinking cheaply, we frugal rootless resting travelers not obligated to anyone or anything but ourselves for a brief while. Wild asparagus was ripe growing along low crude stone walls in terraced white-blossoming almond orchards, the countryside was patrolled by pairs of slow-witted Guardia Civil with alien patent-leather hats and ancient rifles—young recruits from orphanages in those last years of the dictatorship of Francisco Franco. One chilly afternoon, out behind the house a small flock of sheep arrived, and one shepherd, a man much older than I, holding a long stick. I had never labored in anything like that way. I expected that I never would. I poured two small glasses full of Spanish brandy and I went out to meet him, carrying them before me in both hands. He was surprised, but in a formal, dignified way, as befitted converse with a stranger, a foreigner, he was friendly, he drank the brandy slowly holding each sip in his mouth to savor it fully and let it warm him. He had a small cloth bag of possessions and only two dozen or so sheep. As these grazed on the thin grass, one, a ram, he twice cracked casually but hard over the head with the long stick—for what offense I, knowing nothing of sheep, and only beginning to know something of Spain, could not guess. There was about him a kind of calm, an absence of striving, an unmistakable but to me nearly incomprehensible standing apart from the way I knew how to live, and from the way that the people I had met in Madrid lived—workers and shopkeepers in my neighborhood, scholars, writers, the president of a foundation. There could be no hurry in this man's life; nor could I understand the extent, the unremittingness, of his solitude and exposure to life without a roof. On the low, flat-topped mountains nearby, there would be green summer grazing, toward which he was headed. He wore a dark cape over dark clothes; the nights were still cold. "*Ah señor,*" he said, "*No parece usted saber mucho de las dificultades de los pastores ahora. Las cosas han cambiado. Como es extranjero, usted no puede comprender que nuestro Señor viniera alguna vez a estos humildes pueblos...*" "Sir," he said, "you probably do not know much about the difficulties of shepherds these days. Things have changed. And being a foreigner, you can't understand that Our Lord came one time to these humble villages. Yes, it is true. Perhaps where you are from, there is very little sun, or none at all, since, even in summer, so many of you come here to stay in the sun all day at the shores of the sea, women scarcely wearing any clothing. But you are not aware, I believe, that more important than the sun are the footsteps of Our Lord. I have seen it myself, shown in a film, that He rode a donkey through the town of Pedreguer, only a few hours from here by foot." It was as he told me this, holding the glass of brandy on one hand, that twice with whip-quick motion of his stick in his other he rapped the head of the ram, making a sound as if he had struck a stone. He scarcely had looked at the beast; the beast scarcely reacted, and its uncanny unmammalian eyes in any case seemed indifferent, focused single-mindedly on something the shepherd and I could not see, and of far greater importance than we. "Do you travel always on foot?" I asked him. "Always when I am with my flock," he said. "But every year after shearing time I stay a while at my sister's house, and there I have a little motorbike." He smiled suddenly. "I call it Rocinante. Do you know the name?" We were standing behind the rented house, in a patch of open grass among the citrus groves in the thousand-year-old day that contained oranges, sadness, belief, nonbelief, and stories. Another encounter had been offered to me, that I had every reason on that day to accept, to live, and then try to imagine.

7.

My English mentor, dissent- [1973-74]
                er still and anything but
a latter-day Romantic,
                with the drifting Navy Flake
smoke from his pipe would signal
                me toward new directions
where Pound, Oppen, Tomlinson,
                Bunting, but Hardy too, stood
along the lines like statues
                silently repeating their
verses so they could be heard.
                In my tree-shaded student
mornings (my black tea, pen, note-
                book and Turkish cigarettes),
Roethke clambered and sang, he
                had mud on his boots, Jeffers
kept his feelings clean, watched the
                sky without mercy, Rich de-
scended steps against the law,
                Levertov breathlessly prayed
out sensuous invitations,
                whirling metaphors flew from
Ginsburg, at loud group meals my
                young friends argued, laughed and raged
under home-made murals of
                Inferno at New Pisa
in San Francisco and at
                the Basque Hotel, where shepherds
down from the Sierra ate
                sheepless in corners, and on
Saturday mornings Jaime
                de Angulo's singsong strange
accent on radio re-

                        told of bird-people, roaring
monsters, delicate fates or
                        demonic ones, and our crowds
massed, chanted, threw stones to break
                        reactionary windows,
distant war roared and we thought
                        and thought, and could not fly, nor
would my shaking sense of things
                        resolve, my incurable
arrhythmia of feeling.

8.

my illustrations swallow up my thesis

I feel too intensely the omnipresence of all in each, platonically speaking—or psychologically my brain fibres, or the spiritual Light which abides in the brain marrow as visible Light appears to do in sundry rotten mackerel & other *smashy* matters, is of too general an affinity with all things—and tho' it perceives the *difference* of things, yet is eternally pursuing the likenesses, or rather that which is common

bring me two things that seem the very same, & then I am quick enough to shew the difference, even to hair-splitting—but to go on from circle to circle till I break against the shore of my Hearer's patience, or have my Concentricals dashed to nothing by a Snore—that is my ordinary mishap. At Malta, however, no one can charge me with one or the other. I have earned the general character of being a quiet well meaning man, rather dull indeed—& who would have thought, that he had been a *Poet*! 'O very wretched Poetaster, Ma'am! As to the reviews, it is well known, he half ruined himself in paying cleverer fellows than himself to write them' &c—

25 Dec[ember] 1804

He satirized himself, so;
     he lamented—to the self
whom he revised by writing
     his journals—his shattered in-
consolable grief over
     his lost love, his wrong marriage,
and he chided himself for
     failings—for example, his
sloth, or his "Mahometan

                        Superstition—dread as to
the destruction of Paper."
                        While secretary to the
Governor of Malta—his
                        perhaps cowardly attempt
to make an escape from his
                        marriage and a living—he
described this curious dread:
>   I am almost ashamed to confess to myself, what pulling back
>   of Heart I feel whenever I wish to light a candle or kindle a
>   fire with a Hospital or Harbour Report and what a cumulus
>   lie upon my Table, I am not able to conjecture what use they
>   can ever be, and yet trembling lest what I thus destroyed
>   might be of some use, in the way of knowle[d]ge. Thus seems
>   the excess of a good feeling; but it is ridiculous.

Monday Feb[ruary] 11, 1805.

His care for official writs—
                        however useless—seems to
show him at a moment when
                        he even identifies
himself with rule, with the state.

                        His endless thought and writing;
his crises endless, also.
                        His quondam hatred of hot
monarchical sugar-scum;
                        his fear of illiterates
he'd once defended… There'd be
                        no more strenuous pamphlets,
letters, clandestine fireside
                        talk while drying muddy shoes,

/ 25

him quaking, damp, arguing
>   that common people should be
freed from tyranny, hunger,
>   mistaken concepts, drink, jails,
that they should not be punished
>   for ignorance from which they
had had no means of escape.
>   What an eon had passed since
he had preached long last-minute
>   sermons stuffed with chapters and
verses to support his then
>   revolutionary Christ,
he could not let himself feel
>   anguish for the poor as they
desperately tried to cling to
>   slanted bowsprits of the king's
merchants, bankers, noblemen.

>   (And in my time to those of
CEOs, celebrities,
>   marketers, war patriots?)

9.

Samuel Taylor Coleridge,
                    you ask at the edge of all
you have endeavored to think
                    through: "Those Whispers just as you
have fallen or are falling
                    asleep—what are they and whence?"   [4-8 March 1805]

The many that you saw in
                    one, the perhaps reconciled
opposites in their balance:
                    Oneness and Plurality, [13-18 December 1803]
"endless Variety in
                    Identity," multitude   [19-21 October 1803]
and Unity, and your twice-   [13-15 December 1804]
                    recorded fantasy: "I
would make a pilgrimage to
                    the burning sands of Arab-
ia, or &c &
                    c[,] to find the Man
who could explain to me [how]
                    there can be *oneness*, there be-
ing infinite Perceptions."   [November 1799; October 1803]
                    Were irreconcilable
opposites what murmured in
                    the night?—voices of the too
many thoughts that came crowding
                    from within—the too many
English men and women whose
                    cries you could no longer bear?
So perhaps you displaced real
                    suffering and clamor of
the thick human crowd onto

/ 27

                        the appealing green fronds that
need no literacy nor
                        franchise: this is the image
before your mind's eye—lovely
                        "Fern... scattered thick but growing
single"; and still they grow in
                        our unavoidable self-
conscious self-dividedness,
                        our heritages at odds,
our paper trails and trials of
                        spills and slips, they are growing
in our back seats and worn shoes,
                        in our mulch of paychecks, in
our notebooks red-inked from our
                        dialectical bloodstreams,
our desire to reconcile
                        the many and the one, power
and the governed, word and act.

10.

If I successfully tell
            of a few of his and my
representative moments,
            shot through with insoluble
political and also
            poetic dilemmas, then
I have done nothing more than
            compare myself to him with-
out justification; if
            I confine to him what I
tell, I'm merely cutting and
            pasting from detective work
done by someone else. If I
            recount his decline and his
retreat from early powers,
            feelings, ideas, then what I
say may seem only bloodless,
            and anyway will be far
from what poetry is now
            like.

            (Fragmenting itself while
murmuring at a full-length
            mirror, or conditioning
its hair, or failing to raise
            the heavy beams of as yet
uncreated consciousness,
            or running the long lonely
distances, or making the
            audience laugh, or leave, or
intimate, personal and
            linguistically modest

to a fault, or by contrast,
  surreal with lots of flash, gym-
nastic metaphorizing,
  fast-paced non sequiturs, man-
nerisms, and, thrown in some-
  times for the rhetorical
effect, what seems a casual
  "spirituality"—un-
like the fervid expressions
  of frightened faith in writings
by STC himself.) In

   addition, there's the psycho-
logical dimension of
   Coleridge's notebooks, and

anyone who does not re-
   cognize the extent to which
early and intimate re-
   lationships have given a
decisive shape to later
   life is willfully seeking
to be emotionally
   blind; or blinded—I think of
angry men voting for the
   combative false Senator,
using him to justify
   their knee-kick cruelty full
of fear, their crying need for
   enemies... And meanwhile our
early experiences
   and social interactions,

and hot saturating din
            of cold surrounding media
also create in each of
            us what later we will tend
to think is the natural
            way things simply have to be—
to say nothing of the in-
            fluence into us of our
decisive experiences
            of revolutions, social
traumas, judges, police, pain,
            one and another of our
Presidents fastening gold
            medals round the necks of his
war-felons of freedom; of
            new shampoos, of loud lying
for religious money; of
            real stars in their imagined
battles, and real bleeding of
            unimagined bombed persons.

11.

In order to evoke him-
>   self as he wished to be, he
had joined with Wordsworth to draw
>   into their poetry new
subjects from the common life,
>   from fantasy, reverie
and political ideals.
>   But the cabin boy in his
notebooks is perhaps the last
>   object he chose that belonged
to this earlier self that
>   he was leaving behind. Yet
he continued to ponder
>   how to understand spirit,
mind, being. He wrote: "all the
>   subtler parts of one's nature,
must be *solitary*—Man
>   exists herein to himself
& to God alone /—yea, in
>   how much only to God—how
much lies *below* his own"—he
>   uses this word—"Consciousness."   [October 1803]
Awareness. Or as image,
>   earlier: "A River, so
translucent as not to be
>   seen—and yet murmuring—shad-
owy world—& these a Dream /
>   Inchanted River." Well, if   [1802?]
our "nature" is just to be
>   solitary, and our thought
is as "natural" as a
>   river, then what's our social
obligation? I feel the

>   attraction of a psycho-
> logical alibi for
>   not saving the cabin boy…

Here's Coleridge's sense of
                    mind's under-life, recorded
after evidently he
                    had taken a dose of drugs:

Wednesday—Afternoon. Abed—nervous—had noticed the prismatic colours transmitted from the Tumbler—Wordsworth came—I talked with him—he left me alone—I shut my eyes—beauteous spectra of two colors, orange and violet—then of green, which immediately changed to Peagreen, & then actually *grew* to my eye into a beautiful moss, the same as is on the mantle-piece at Grasmere.—abstract Ideas—& unconscious Links!!

                                                            [1801]

And now unconsciously I
                    choose him by intuition
merely; yet also, I am
                    sure, in order to evoke
in myself some aspect I
                    sense is either wanting or
must be strengthened before I
                    can proceed any further.
Or because I am frightened
                    and STC gives me his
permission to retreat? Un-

                    deniable resemblance
links his moment with our own.

                        Politically, even
if not poetically.
                        The two second-hand volumes
of his notebooks that I bought   [1973?]
                        (1794 to
1804): I did not
                        then understand how we use
what we read. I was drawn, in
                        awe, to the pages of in-
numerable names of plants,
                        above all, wildflowers (not   [1800]
written in Coleridge's
                        hand but in that of his, so
he thought, real love, "Asra," (this
                        Sara was a Hutchinson).
Unable to comprehend
                        much of Coleridge's thought,
of my time so much, as he
                        was of his—ages of ex-
cess, hope then horror, hope *and*
                        horror—I went outside, where
some of my flower books are,
                        to study the green fern-texts.   [2004-05]

A Note on the Text

Source texts from *Coleridge's Notebooks: A Selection*, edited by Seamus Perry (Oxford University Press, 2002); *The Notebooks of Samuel Taylor Coleridge*, edited by Kathleen Coburn, Volume I: 1794-1804 (Princeton University Press, 1957). Samuel Taylor Coleridge = 1772-1834. Coleridge's marriage to Sarah Fricker left him bitter and irresponsible; he believed, but perhaps unreasonably, that the love he then conceived for Sara Hutchinson, the sister of Wordsworth's wife Mary, would have been requited had he not already been married. William Wordsworth = 1770-1850.

www.ingramcontent.com/pod-product-compliance
Lightning Source LLC
Chambersburg PA
CBHW022346040426
42449CB00006B/742